Date: 8/17/17

J BIO DRAPER
Shea, Therese,
Sharon Draper : author /

JUNIOR
BIOGRAPHIES

SHARON DRAPER

AUTHOR

Therese M. Shea

Enslow Publishing
101 W. 23rd Street
Suite 240
New York, NY 10011
USA

enslow.com

ambassador A person who travels to another country to represent a group.

career A job that someone does for a long time.

cerebral palsy A disease that causes a person to have problems moving and speaking.

challenge Something that is hard to do; also, asking someone to do something hard.

dare To tell someone to do something to show that you are brave.

disability A condition that limits a person's mental or physical abilities.

literary Having to do with books.

master's degree A degree or title given to a student by a college or university usually after one or two years of additional study following a bachelor's degree.

translate To change words from one language to another.

CONTENTS

CHAPTER 1

AUTHOR AND EDUCATOR

Sharon Draper has had two **careers**: teaching and writing. To her, they are linked. "I write because I teach," she said. Only a teacher who understood her students' lives and needs could become the author whose books would connect with them so well.

> Sharon Says:
>
> **"I was probably born to be a teacher. As a child, I taught my dolls, my dogs, and the kids next door."**

A LIFELONG LOVE OF LITERATURE

Sharon first started writing for others after a student **dared** her to enter a contest.

But it was her love of reading growing up that made her want to be an English teacher and, later, an author.

Sharon loved books from a very young age and was glad her parents encouraged her reading.

Sharon thanked her parents for giving her a love of books.

Sharon was born August 21, 1952, in Cleveland, Ohio. Her father was a hotel waiter named Victor Mills and her mother, Catherine, worked at a newspaper. Sharon was the oldest of three children. Books filled their home, and Catherine read to the children every night. "I inhaled books and knowledge," Sharon said of that time.

FUN FACT

Sharon's books talk about issues that young people face today, especially African Americans.

Reading was one of Sharon's favorite things to do as a child.

CHAPTER 2
STUDENT AND TEACHER

Her parents also encouraged her in school. They taught her that she could reach any goal through hard work. She did well in her classes.

Sharon wanted to be like her fifth grade teacher, Kathadaza Mann. Mann taught about black history before most teachers did. She taught Sharon to speak her mind as well.

Sharon excelled in high school and graduated as a National Merit Scholar. She attended Pepperdine

FUN FACT

Sharon's book *Copper Sun* was chosen for an international reading project. Students in the United States, Nigeria, and Ghana read the book and shared their ideas about it.

Sharon grew up in Cleveland, Ohio. After attending college in Malibu, California, she returned to Ohio.

Sharon Says:

"I am so proud to be a teacher. I'm proud of my colleagues, 3 million of us, who strive every day in the classrooms across the country to make a difference in the lives of students."

University in Malibu, California, and graduated with a degree in English in 1971. Sharon then attended Miami University of Ohio, where she earned a **master's degree** in 1974.

Sharon became an English teacher in Cincinnati Public Schools. She was a tough but fair teacher. She encouraged her students to connect the books they read with their lives and current events.

A CHALLENGING TEACHER

Sharon **challenged** her students to become better writers. Seniors had to write a research paper that became known

While earning her master's degree, Sharon married her husband, Larry Draper, who was also a teacher. The couple has four children.

as the "Draper Paper." Students who passed were given T-shirts that said: "I Survived the Draper Paper."

Sharon's teaching methods were noticed. In 1997 she was named Ohio Teacher of the Year and then US Teacher of the Year. Sharon toured the United States as a teaching **ambassador**. She spoke to other teachers about how to improve and to communities about how they can support teachers.

Former President Bill Clinton said of Sharon Draper: "For 27 years she has inspired students with her passion for literature and life. Sharon Draper is more than a credit to her profession, she is a true blessing to the children she has taught."

CHAPTER 3
THE AUTHOR EMERGES

Sharon was not just challenging her students. She was challenging herself through writing. She won a short story contest for *Ebony* magazine in 1990 after a student dared her to enter. It made her want to write more. She decided to write something her students would want to read.

It was not easy to find time to write, but Sharon worked at night and on the weekends. It took her a year

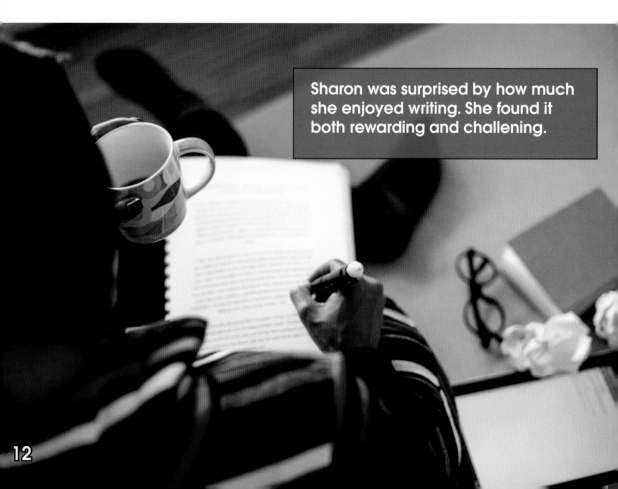

Sharon was surprised by how much she enjoyed writing. She found it both rewarding and challenging.

to finish her first young adult novel, *Tears of a Tiger*. The hard work was not over, though. Sharon had to send the book to twenty-five publishers before it was finally published in 1994.

WRITING FOR YOUNG ADULTS

Sharon used her knowledge of her students' lives when writing *Tears of a Tiger*. She also made the writing interesting, using journal entries, school papers, and letters to tell the story. The novel included serious topics such as alcohol and drug use because students deal with those issues every day.

Young readers were drawn to the book as well as to the African American role models in it. *Tears of a Tiger* won the 1995 American Library Association Best Book for Young Adults. Sharon won the Coretta Scott King Genesis Award as an outstanding African American author.

Many of Sharon's twenty-eight books are best sellers.

She went on to write two more books about the *Tears of a Tiger* characters.

Another publishing company asked Sharon to write for younger readers. She wrote a mystery called *Ziggy and the Black Dinosaurs*, which came out in November 1994. Sharon wrote five more books about Ziggy and his friends. They teach lessons about life and history.

Later, Sharon met a young girl who asked her to write books for "girls like me." So, Sharon wrote a popular series about a fourth grader named Sassy.

Sharon has noted that many children stop reading for fun when they are in middle school. That is why she writes for this age group as well as young adults.

Sharon Says:

"**Perhaps reading about the difficulties of others will act like an armor and protect my readers from the personal tragedies of their own lives.**"

A teacher once told Sharon that the only book one of her students had ever read completely was *Tears of a Dragon*. Sharon has made a difference in many lives through teaching and writing. Young people are drawn to

Sharon's favorite part of her job is knowing that she is writing something students want to read!

her work because they see themselves and their friends in them—and not just young African American people, but also those with **disabilities**.

Sharon's book *Out of My Mind*, released in 2010, focused on a girl with **cerebral palsy** and the challenges she faced growing up. The book remained on the *New York Times* Best Sellers list for nearly two years. It won numerous awards and was **translated** into several languages.

CHAPTER 4
HONORING SHARON

Sharon Draper has been honored at the White House six times. She was chosen to speak at the Library of Congress National Book Festival Gala in Washington, DC, and to represent the United States in Moscow at the Russian Book Festival.

The awards for Sharon's work keep coming in, not only for individual books but for her body of work. In 2015, she was honored by the American Library Association with the Margaret A. Edwards Award for lifetime **literary** achievement.

Sharon Says:

"I write because I care about young people."

STILL WRITING

Sharon says on her website: "I love to write; words flow easily from my fingertips." With more than twenty-five books published

Sharon no longer teaches. Now, she inspires young minds through her books.

so far, her love of writing—and young people—is shown by her words.

Despite her success, it's doubtful that Sharon will slow down any time soon. Literature and education are far too important to her. She wants to give kids something they want to read. She also wants to give them something to which they can relate. She hopes to inspire others to love reading and writing as much as she does.

In 2014, Sharon attended the National Book Awards.

TIMELINE

1952 Sharon Mills is born August 21 in Cleveland, Ohio.

1971 Sharon graduates from Pepperdine University.

1974 Sharon graduates from Miami University of Ohio.

1990 Sharon wins a short story contest for Ebony magazine.

1994 *Tears of a Tiger* and *Ziggy and the Black Dinosaurs* are published.

1995 *Tears of a Tiger* wins the 1995 American Library Association Best Book for Young Adults.

1997 Sharon is named Ohio Teacher of the Year and US Teacher of the Year.

2006 *Copper Sun* is published.

2009 The first Sassy book is published.

2010 *Out of My Mind* is published.

2015 Sharon is given the Margaret A. Edwards Award for lifetime literary achievement.

BOOKS

Draper, Sharon M. *Out of My Mind.* New York, NY: Atheneum Books for Young Readers, 2012.

Draper, Sharon M. *Stella by Starlight.* New York, NY: Simon & Schuster, 2015.

Kumar, Lisa. *Something About the Author.* Detroit, MI: Gale, 2013.

WEBSITES

Notable Biographies
notablebiographies.com/news/Ca-Ge/Draper-Sharon.html
Find out more about Sharon's life.

Scholastic Books
scholastic.com/teachers/contributor/sharon-m-draper
Read a short biography of Sharon.

Sharon Draper
sharondraper.com
Check out a list of Sharon's books here.

Index

Published in 2017 by Enslow Publishing, LLC.
101 W. 23rd Street, Suite 240, New York, NY 10011

Copyright © 2017 by Enslow Publishing, LLC.

Library of Congress Cataloging-in-Publication Data:
Names: Shea, Therese, author.
Title: Sharon Draper : author / Therese M. Shea.
Description: New York, NY : Enslow Publishing, 2017. | Series: Junior biographies | Includes bibliographical references and index.
Identifiers: LCCN 2016020789| ISBN 9780766081901 (library bound) | ISBN 9780766081888 (pbk.) | ISBN 9780766081895 (6-pack)
Subjects: LCSH: Draper, Sharon M. (Sharon Mills)—Juvenile literature. | African American women authors—Biography—Juvenile literature.
Classification: LCC PS3554.R24 Z82 2016 | DDC 813/.54 [B]—dc23
LC record available at https://lccn.loc.gov/2016020789

Printed in China

To Our Readers: We have done our best to make sure all websites in this book were active and appropriate when we went to press. However, the author and the publisher have no control over and assume no liability for the material available on those websites or on any websites they may link to. Any comments or suggestions can be sent by e-mail to customerservice@enslow.com.

Photo Credits: Cover, pp. 1, 21 Robin Marchant/Getty Images; p. 4 © AP Images; p. 6 (top) Theodore Trimmer/Shutterstock.com; p. 7 Stockbyte/Thinkstock; p. 9 Henryk Sadura/Moment/Getty Images; p. 10 Wolffystyle/Wikimedia Commons/File:Pepperdine University Malibu Canyon Entrance Gate.JPG/CC BY-SA 3.0; p. 11 Stephen Jaffe/AFP/Getty Images; p. 12 Peter Bernik/Shutterstock.com; p. 14 Kalamazoo Public Library/flickr.com/photos/kalamazoopubliclibrary/2926881686; p. 16 Kalamazoo Public Library/flickr.com/photos/kalamazoopubliclibrary/2926884008; 19 Jeffrey Beall/Wikimedia Commons/File:Sharon Draper.JPG/CC BY-SA 3.0; back cover, interior pages (curves graphic) Alena Kazlouskaya/Shutterstock.com; interior pages (book) Faenkova Elena/Shutterstock.com.